save the . . .
LIONS

by **Sarah L. Thomson**
with an introduction
by **Chelsea Clinton**

PHILOMEL

PHILOMEL BOOKS
An imprint of Penguin Random House LLC, New York

First published in the United States of America by Philomel Books,
an imprint of Penguin Random House LLC, 2023

Visit us online at penguinrandomhouse.com.

Library of Congress Cataloging-in-Publication Data is available.

Printed in the United States of America

ISBN 9780593404058 (hardcover)
ISBN 9780593404065 (paperback)

1st Printing

LSCC

Edited by Talia Benamy and Jill Santopolo
Design by Lily Qian
Text set in Calisto MT Pro

save the . . .

save the . . .
BLUE WHALES

save the . . .
ELEPHANTS

save the . . .
FROGS

save the . . .
GIRAFFES

save the . . .
GORILLAS

save the . . .
LIONS

save the . . .
POLAR BEARS

save the . . .
TIGERS

save the . . .
WHALE SHARKS

Dear Reader,

When I was around your age, my favorite animals were dinosaurs and elephants. I wanted to know everything I could about triceratopses, stegosauruses and other dinosaurs that had roamed our earth millions of years ago. Elephants, though, captured my curiosity and my heart. The more I learned about the largest animals on land today, the more I wanted to do to help keep them and other endangered species safe forever.

So I joined organizations working around the world to support endangered species and went to our local zoo to learn more about conservation efforts close to home (thanks to my parents and grandparents). I tried to learn as much as I could about how we can ensure animals and plants don't go extinct like the dinosaurs, especially since it's the choices that we're making that pose the greatest threat to their lives today.

The choices we make don't have to be huge to make

a real difference. When I was in elementary school, I used to cut up the plastic rings around six-packs of soda, glue them to brightly colored construction paper (purple was my favorite) and hand them out to whomever would take one in a one-girl campaign to raise awareness about the dangers that plastic six-pack rings posed to marine wildlife around the world. I learned about that from a book—*50 Simple Things Kids Can Do to Save the Earth*—which helped me understand that you're never too young to make a difference and that we all can change the world. I hope that this book will inform and inspire you to help save this and other endangered species. There are tens of thousands of species that are currently under threat, with more added every year. We have the power to save those species, and with your help, we can.

Sincerely,

Chelsea Clinton

save the . . .
LIONS

CONTENTS

-- -- -- -- -- -- -- -- -- -- -- -- -- --

SAVANNAS, FORESTS, AND DESERTS:
WHERE LIONS LIVE

If you lived in North America around one hundred thousand years ago, you would have wanted to be careful going for a stroll across a grassy plain. You might have met an American lion. If you'd lived in Europe about the same time and went for a hike in the forest, you could have come face-to-face with a cave lion.

But these two kinds of lions went extinct about ten thousand years ago. Today, you can only find lions in Africa and Asia.

(You might have heard of mountain lions—they live in North, South, and Central America. But they are not true lions, even though they have "lion" in the name. They're also called cougars, pumas, or catamounts.)

A Place to Find Food

You might already know that lions are big cats. Like all cats, from lions to tigers to leopards to house cats, lions are hunters. They choose places to live where it's easy for them to find prey.

A hungry lion will eat almost anything it can find, including insects or lizards or ostrich eggs or crocodiles or baby elephants. But a lion's most common prey are herbivores, like gazelles, wildebeests, and zebras. These

Grasslands with a few trees are also called savannas. They provide food, water, and shelter for lions.

plant-eaters munch on grass, leaves, and brush, and they live where they can find plenty of this food year-round. That means places that are warm or hot most of the time and dry but not too dry.

If a lion has to, it will make a home almost anywhere it can scratch out a living. Lions manage to survive in most habitats, except in the driest deserts or in thick tropical rain forests near the equator.

But there are some types of habitats that lions prefer. Grasslands with scattered trees are perfect for them. Forests and places with thickets and dense brush are also good. There's lots of food in these places for the animals that lions like to hunt. And there are also good spots for female lions to make dens that will keep their cubs safe.

If you add in a water source—a pond, stream, river, or lake—and you have the excellent habitat for a lion: a place where it can find everything it needs to survive.

African lions can be found in Africa south of the Sahara. When it comes to Asiatic lions, there is only one spot where they still exist in the wild—the Gir Forest of northwest India. More than half of the Asiatic lions left live in this forest. The rest can be found in zoos.

Africa or Asia, savanna or forest—wherever a lion lives, it's going to be hot. One way these big cats handle the heat is to rest a lot. Lions spend hours and hours asleep, often in a shady spot if they can find one. They are most active when it's a little cooler, during the night or at dawn or dusk.

That's when they go hunting.

Big Cats Hunt Big Prey

Lions tend to hunt big prey like wildebeests because they are big themselves—the second biggest cats on Earth. Only tigers are larger (and not by much).

A full-grown African lion is between three and a half to four feet tall at the shoulder, and it can be ten feet long from its nose to the tip of its tail. A big male lion can weigh five hundred pounds, a bit heavier than a Shetland pony. A female lion, a lioness, is usually a little smaller.

Asiatic lions aren't quite as big as African lions. A big male could grow to a little over four hundred pounds, and the longest one ever measured was nine feet. A male Asiatic lion also has a thinner mane than an African lion. You can usually see his ears poking through the fur.

A male lion is larger than a lioness, and males also have manes. These big ruffs of fur make them look big and threatening to other males.

Other than that, Asiatic and African lions are pretty much the same, except for one thing—a loose flap of skin that runs along the length of their bellies. Asiatic lions always have this flap. It shows up very rarely in their African relatives.

A big cat like a lion needs to eat a lot—about twenty pounds of meat a day is a good amount. But if it gets the chance, a lion might stuff itself with up to a hundred pounds of meat at a time. You'd need to eat four hundred hamburgers (minus the buns, but you can add ketchup if you want) if you were to do the same thing.

A lion chows down like this because it might not get to eat the next day, or the one after that. Hunting is hard work, and lions aren't always successful. On average, prey will get away from a lion eight or nine times out of ten. Lions are sometimes forced to go a week between meals.

A lion can sprint about thirty miles per hour—a little faster than a car going down a

An Asiatic lion prowls through the Gir Forest of India.

neighborhood street. But it can't keep up that speed for long. Most prey can run faster and longer than a lion.

So a lion uses its habitat to gain an advantage over its prey. It might hide behind thick bushes or in a streambed or among the roots of trees, waiting to ambush its next meal. Or it might use grass to help it stay hidden.

Have you ever watched a pet cat sneak across a lawn, trying to get close to a bird or a chipmunk or a squirrel? It crouches, belly close to the ground, and inches along so slowly it hardly seems to be moving at all.

Big or small, it doesn't matter—one cat stalking prey looks a lot like another.

A lion will do the same thing. The short grass of a lawn doesn't do much to keep that pet cat hidden, but the tall, yellow-brown grass of a savanna does a superb job of hiding a hunting lion. The lion's tawny coat keeps it perfectly camouflaged. Then, once a lion gets close enough to its prey, it will make a quick dash, hoping to grab it.

If the prey gets away, a lion has another way to get food. Lions often scavenge. They steal food from any other hunter that has made a kill. Leopards, cheetahs, hyenas, and African wild dogs all live and hunt where lions do, and if a lion gets a chance, it will scare off the other predator and finish eating its meal. (A pack of hyenas will sometimes do the same thing to a lion. Overall, though, lions get more food from hyenas than hyenas get from them.)

But when there's nothing to scavenge, a lion has to rely on hunting. And as difficult as that might be, lions have one great advantage that other big cats don't have.

A lion can hunt in a group called a pride.

2

LIFE IN A PRIDE: WHAT LIONS ARE LIKE

There are cats all over the world—ocelots in the jungles of South America, caracals in the deserts of the Middle East, lynx in the forests of North America, tigers in the swamps of India, and leopards in the woodlands of Africa.

Cats can be small enough to curl up on your lap or as big as a Siberian tiger. But all cats have a few things in common. They are carnivores who must eat meat to survive. They have five toes on their front paws and four on the back, between twenty-eight and thirty teeth inside their mouths, and a powerful bite. And they live alone. Mothers raise their kittens or cubs to adulthood, but after that, cats live by themselves.

Except for lions. Lions are the only kind of cat that live, hunt, eat, and raise their young in a pride.

Family Life

A pride of African lions may have as few as three lions or as many as forty. Most prides fall somewhere in the middle. There are usually several female lions in a pride along with their cubs. The females are often related. They may be mothers, daughters, sisters, or cousins to each other.

A pride has either one male or a small group of males, perhaps two or three. A group like this is called a coalition. (Say it like this: co-al-IH-shun.) Sometimes the males in a coalition are brothers or cousins who grew up in the same pride, but they are not always related.

And the males and the females of a pride are *never* from the same family. This is important, because the males are the fathers of all the cubs in the pride. If they were closely related to the females, their cubs would not be healthy.

Asiatic lions live in groups as well, but their prides don't include males and females living together. Males most often spend their time in coalitions of two, and females and cubs live in their own prides. The males and females come together only to mate.

Why do lions live in prides when no other cats do so? Being in a pride makes life easier for lions in several ways.

The first is hunting. Males may grab a meal now and then, but in a pride, the females do most of the hunting. The lionesses cooperate to bring down prey.

Several female lions might creep up on the same gazelle or zebra, moving slowly and silently through the grass. If the animal spots one lioness and bolts, it may run straight into the jaws of another. Or some of the smaller, younger females might chase prey toward older members of the pride who are lurking and waiting to ambush it.

To kill small prey, like a rodent or a reptile, a lioness will bite it on the back of the neck, slicing through the spine. With larger prey, a lioness often clamps her strong jaws over the prey's muzzle or throat, cutting off its breath.

Hunting in a group means a much better

chance of bringing down prey. Lions who hunt alone catch their prey about 8 percent of the time. Hunting with others brings that success rate closer to 20 percent—and even higher if the hunters manage to creep close to the prey without being seen or heard or smelled.

Once prey is brought down, the pride shares in the meal. Males usually eat first, and then the females get their share. Cubs eat last, with the

Hunting together means eating together. This pride shares a warthog they've killed.

biggest ones getting the first chance at the food.

Male lions may not do much to keep the pride fed, but they also have an important role. A pride controls a certain area of land, or territory. Males spend much of their time patrolling their territory, on the alert for any threat.

What are they watching for? There aren't many animals who can threaten a full-grown lion. An elephant might trample a lion, and a giraffe can do a lot of damage with a well-placed kick. A large crocodile could injure a lion as well. But on the whole, lions are pretty safe—except for one danger.

Other lions.

The biggest threat to a pride of lions is other lions who want to move into their territory— male lions in particular. Males without a pride of their own are always on the lookout for a pride that they might take over.

A single male, or a coalition of two or three males, might linger on the outskirts of a pride's territory for a few days or weeks. Then perhaps they'll move closer. The male or males of the pride will try to frighten the newcomers off. If that doesn't work, it's time for a fight.

The sharp claws and long teeth that are so deadly to prey are just as dangerous to another lion.

If the pride's male, or males, wins, the invaders are killed or driven away. If the invaders win, they will stay with the lionesses of the pride.

One of the first things the new males will do is kill any cubs who are too young to run away. They'll do this because they are driven to mate with the females themselves and sire their own cubs. It seems cruel, but it doesn't do a male lion any good to protect cubs who are not his own. A lioness may try to defend her cubs, but she won't have much of a chance against a bigger, stronger male.

That's why the males of a pride are so important. The females rely on the males to keep other male lions away and make sure their cubs are safe. A female in a pride is twice as likely to raise a cub to adulthood than a female who is living on her own. Life in a pride gives a cub its best chance at growing up.

On Their Own

A pride can make life easier and safer for a lion—but even so, not every lion spends its whole life in a group. Lions who don't live in a pride are called nomads. Most males, and a few females, will spend a part of their lives as nomads.

If a female nomad meets up with male nomads, they may form a new pride together. Or a female nomad might join a pride that already exists.

Male nomads may wander by themselves, or they may join with one or two other males to form a coalition. As they grow stronger and more experienced, they'll probably try to find a pride that they can take over.

And a few lions never join prides at all. This is most likely to happen in areas where prey is scarce and there isn't enough to share. About fifty lions live in the Samburu National Reserve in northern Kenya, and none of them live in prides. Each lion—male or female— hunts for itself. Each mother raises her cubs alone.

How to Speak Lion

Whether they live in a pride or alone, lions must communicate with other lions. One way they do so is, of course, by roaring.

A lion's roar can be heard three to five miles away. If a lion was roaring at one end of Central Park in New York City, you could stand at the other end and hear it easily. And that's good, because the roar carries a message to other lions. It's a way to claim the pride's territory and to warn outsiders to keep their distance.

Lions are able to tell the difference between a roar from a pridemate and one from a stranger. They can also tell the difference between a big group of lions roaring and a smaller one.

Lions make other sounds as well. They growl or snarl to warn off an intruder or tell a pesky cub to move along. They can hiss or meow just like a pet cat, and they also make a sound called a puff, a bit like the sound you might make if you were trying not to let a sneeze out. It's a friendly sound to let other lions know that all is well.

Sound isn't the only way lions communicate. They also mark objects with their scent. A lion might rub its muzzle against a tree, just like a pet cat rubs against a chair or a couch or your leg. This leaves its smell on the surface it touches. The lion also rakes its paws against the ground, ripping up grass and leaving scent behind. And male lions spray urine over grass or bushes or dirt. It's like the lion is slapping up signs wherever it goes, telling the world—especially other lions—where it has been. Those signs mark exactly where the lion's territory begins and ends.

Lions also use touch to stay connected with their pride. When pridemates meet, they will rub their faces and heads together. And lions, especially female lions, spend time licking and grooming each other with their long tongues. If you've ever been licked by a pet cat, you know how prickly their tongues are. A lion's tongue is even more prickly, with tiny barbs all over. The barbs are so sharp that a lion can lick fur or feathers off its prey and meat right off a bone. When lions lick each other, the tongue washes dirt and dust away and combs the fur as well.

Mother lions also lick and groom their cubs, of course. Keeping cubs clean and safe is a lioness's job.

For a cub, getting licked by its mother is like getting a bath and having its hair brushed at the same time.

Growing Up Lion

The female lions of a pride often give birth at about the same time, and most have between one and four cubs in a litter. When a lioness is ready to have her babies, she moves away from her pride and finds a den of her own.

A cub weighs three or four pounds when it is born, about half the weight of a newborn human. Cubs huddle close to their mother and drink her milk, growing stronger day by day. At around three weeks, their teeth come in, and they start to nibble at solid food a few weeks later. By then the mother is usually ready to lead them back to their pride, where they will grow up alongside other cubs. Even though the young cubs can gnaw on meat or bones, they'll keep nursing from their mothers—and sometimes from other females in the pride—until they are about six or eight months old.

Just like you might play with your friends or siblings or cousins, cubs play, wrestle, and chase their pridemates. They may play tug-of-war with a bone or a tough piece of meat. They stalk other cubs and pounce on them, and they might do the same with the twitching tail of

A cub who leaps on a pridemate may grow up to tackle a full-grown gazelle or zebra.

an adult lion. Play isn't just for fun. It helps the cubs grow strong muscles, and it lets them practice hunting.

It's not all playtime, though—cubs also need to learn to actually hunt. They follow their mothers on hunting trips, and female lions may even bring down prey but let the cubs finish the kill.

By the time they are about two years old, cubs know enough to hunt and fend for themselves. That's good because the young males are now old and big enough to be a threat to the males of their own pride. Their fathers will force them to leave, and they'll become nomads until (if they are lucky) they form a new pride or take over one that already exists.

Female lions, on the other hand, usually stay in the pride where they were born. But now and then, especially if prey is scarce, they may be forced to leave as well.

Alone or in prides, young lions face a world full of many dangers. In 1950, there were about five hundred thousand lions living in the wild across Africa. Today there are only around twenty thousand.

What about Asiatic lions? In 2015, scientists counted 523 of them in the Gir Forest. Five years later that number had increased to 674. Any increase in the number of lions is good . . . but 674 lions is still a pretty small number for an animal that once lived all over India and the Middle East.

What has made this world such a difficult one for lions to live in?

3

HUNTING AND HABITAT: WHY ARE LIONS ENDANGERED?

The International Union for Conservation of Nature (IUCN) keeps track of animal species all over the world and notes which ones are in danger. Their Red List of Threatened Species™ puts animals into seven different categories:

Least Concern: This animal is doing all right. There are enough healthy animals to have enough healthy babies to keep the species going.

Near Threatened: This animal is not in trouble yet, but there are danger signs. It may become Vulnerable, Endangered, or Critically Endangered soon.

Vulnerable: There are not many of this animal left, its numbers are falling, and it can live only in certain small areas. It is at risk of extinction.

Endangered: This animal is at *high risk* of extinction.

Critically Endangered: This animal is at *very high risk* of extinction.

Extinct in the Wild: This animal lives only in captivity. There are none left in the wild.

Extinct: This animal is gone forever.

On the Red List, African lions are in the Vulnerable category. Asiatic lions are Endangered. What dangers are lions facing?

Hunting the Hunters

There are very few predators who are a danger to lions. Leopards and hyenas will sometimes hunt lion cubs if their parents are not nearby to protect them. And male lions, of course, may kill cubs if they take over a pride. But there is only one kind of hunter who will target a full-grown lion—and that is a human being.

In India, it's against the law to hunt Asiatic lions. But in some of the African countries where lions live—like Zimbabwe, Tanzania, Mozambique, Namibia, Cameroon, and South Africa—hunting lions is perfectly legal as long as hunters follow the rules set down by the government of that country and pay a lot of money. Hunters pay thousands of dollars to safari companies who provide them with places to stay, food to eat, guides to take them out into the wilderness, and the chance to shoot a lion.

If the hunter does kill a lion, they often have the skin made into a rug or get the lion's head stuffed so that it can be hung on the wall as a trophy. That's why this kind of hunting is called "trophy hunting."

Displaying the head or skin of a lion is a way for a hunter to show everyone that they've killed a large and dangerous animal.

Some people believe that no one should be allowed to hunt lions at all. Others claim that trophy hunting can actually be good for lions—not the ones who are killed, of course, but for the species as a whole. How could that be true?

Well, some of the money from trophy hunting is used to keep up parks and preserves where lions and other animals can live. It also helps to pay the salaries of rangers who keep the animals safe. And hunting can thin out lion populations in areas where they get too crowded. Too many lions in one place will eat too much prey and make life difficult for other predators.

Maybe you agree that trophy hunting could be a good idea. Or maybe you think it ought to be stopped entirely. Either way, there's actually a much bigger threat to lions. That is illegal hunting, or poaching.

Lions are often hunted and killed for their bones, teeth, and claws. Their claws and teeth can be made into jewelry. Bones can be ground into powder, which many people believe works as a kind of medicine. (It doesn't.) The powder can also be used to make a drink called "tiger wine." Tiger wine is expensive and rare, and it makes people feel rich and important to drink it. (As you can guess from the name, tiger wine is supposed to contain powder made from tiger bones, but tigers have become even more endangered than African lions. Often it's easier for poachers to go after lions than tigers.)

Poachers risk their lives and break the law to kill lions because others are willing to pay a lot of money for these body parts. A single lion skeleton can be sold for around three thousand dollars.

People who kill lions for money don't follow the rules. They don't pay money that helps support safe places for lions to live. They don't care if there are too many or too few lions in the area where they are hunting. They just kill as many lions as they can find.

A poacher who goes after a lion with a gun is a pretty obvious threat. But there are other people who become a threat to lions just by moving into spaces the lions once claimed as their own.

Where Have All the Habitats Gone?

Every living thing on Earth, from a kid to an earthworm to a lion to a coral reef, needs a habitat that provides for all of its needs. Think of your house or apartment. To make that place a good habitat for you, there should be food in the fridge and in the cupboards. Water should come out of the faucet. It shouldn't be too hot or too cold inside, so you stay pretty comfortable. Walls and doors and windows should keep you safe from dangerous weather and anything else that might hurt you.

A house or apartment is a good habitat for a kid. A savanna with a stream, plenty of gazelles or zebras to hunt, and bushes or thickets to hide in makes a great habitat for a lion.

But those habitats are becoming harder and harder to find because people take over the land where lions once lived.

People need land to build houses, stores, apartment buildings, factories, roads, and more. They plow the land to plant crops. Or

Big cats need big spaces. It's impossible to protect lions without protecting their habitats.

they fence it off to make pastures where cows, goats, or sheep can graze. Lions and the wild animals they hunt are left with fewer and fewer habitats to call their own.

In 1970, there were 3.6 billion people on Earth. Today there are 7.8 billion. It won't be long before that number reaches 8 billion.

As those billions of people all try to find places to live, water to drink, and food to eat, they build their homes and raise their crops and pasture their animals and make their roads closer and closer to the spaces wild animals like lions have left.

Two Species Too Close Together

With the human population growing larger and larger, more and more people are moving near or even into the wilderness where the remaining lions make their homes. They not only take up the lions' space—they also eat the lions' food. A good number of people rely on hunting to provide for their families. What do they hunt? A lot of the same animals that lions prefer as their prey.

When lions and humans go after the same prey, there's less for everybody to eat. The number of large herbivores—that's plant-eaters who make good prey for big hunters like lions—has dropped by half in East Africa and by even more than that in West Africa. In the Gir Forest, the news is better for Asiatic lions—the population of large herbivores there is slowly rising.

When there are fewer prey, hungry lions have to travel farther looking for food. They may start looking for it in new places, maybe the pens where humans keep cows, goats, or sheep.

A hungry lion doesn't see much of a difference between a wild zebra and a cow, or between a goat and a gazelle. It just sees a meal on hooves.

And if a lion kills a rancher's animals, that rancher sees a threat to their family's survival. Many react by hunting down the lion or by setting out poisoned meat that any nearby lion

A lioness feasts on a cow she's hunted.

will eat. Poisoning has been known to wipe out entire prides.

It's easy to understand a rancher wanting to keep their animals safe. But tracking down and killing a single lion—or even a pride—doesn't do much to end a problem that is actually caused by humans and lions living too close together.

And it's not only humans who are the problem. As lions spend more time near towns and villages, they come into contact with dogs, who may spread diseases to them. Distemper is a common disease among dogs, and it can be deadly to lions.

All lions are at risk when they live too close to people (and to dogs). Asiatic lions are even more at risk than African ones. The Gir Forest is the only place left where these lions live in the wild. They can't simply leave that habitat if humans come too near—there's nowhere else for them to go.

It's hard to imagine a world where there is no space left for lions. But we are coming closer and closer to a time when that may be true.

Luckily, some people are working to make sure that doesn't happen.

LION GUARDIANS:
WHO HAS BEEN SAVING LIONS?

Most of the problems that make life hard for lions have been caused by human beings. So if we all want to live in a world with lions in it, human beings will have to find ways to make things better.

The Nawabs of Junagadh

In the 1800s, Asiatic lions were disappearing all over India. Their habitats were shrinking, and they were under threat from hunters who loved the thrill and triumph of being able to kill a big and dangerous animal.

As the century drew to a close, the only remaining lions in India were in the Gir Forest. Most of that forest was in the royal state of Junagadh.

At that time, India was ruled by the British government. But in parts of the country, royal families still had some control over their own states. These princes, or nawabs, had the power to decide who could hunt within their borders, especially when it came to trophy animals like leopards, tigers, and lions.

In 1879, the sixth nawab of Junagadh, Mahbatkhanji II, realized that Asiatic lions were close to extinction. He banned the hunting of them in Junagadh without his permission.

Later nawabs continued the same protections, making Junagadh one of the earliest places to protect an animal not just because it was useful to humans, but for its own sake. In the Gir Forest, lions had a right to exist simply for being lions.

The ninth nawab of Junagadh, Mahbatkhanji III, was known for his love of animals, especially dogs and, of course, Asiatic lions. When India gained its independence from Britain in 1947, it split into the two countries of India and Pakistan. Mahbatkhanji III tried to make Junagadh into a part of Pakistan. When his plan failed, he was forced to flee from India, taking two hundred of his dogs with him. As he left, he is said to have looked over the Gir Forest and murmured, "Who will protect my lions now?"

The ninth nawab, Mahbatkhanji III.

Junagadh remained in India and in time became part of the state of Gujarat. In 1965, the Indian government made the Gir Forest into a sanctuary to ensure that the remaining lions could live in safety. Thanks to the nawabs of Junagadh, there were still lions there to protect.

Safe from Hunters

Just as the nawabs of Junagadh understood, we can't protect lions without protecting their habitats. Two photographers, a husband and wife named Dereck and Beverly Joubert, have done just that.

The Jouberts have spent their careers making films about the animals that live throughout Africa, including big cats like lions and leopards. They learned about the Selinda Game

Reserve in Botswana, a preserve where hunting was allowed by law. Lions lived there—or at least they once had. So many had been killed that only two remained, a lioness and her grown daughter.

The Jouberts asked for donations to raise money, and in 2006, they paid a fee that allowed them the right to control hunting in Selinda. They made the choice to keep hunters out entirely in order to protect the wildlife there, including the last two remaining lions.

Then two male lions swam across a river to make Selinda their home. They formed a pride with the two females. Both lionesses had cubs, six in all. Since hunting was no longer allowed in Selinda, there was plenty of prey for the brand-new pride. More and more cubs were born, and as the male cubs grew up, they left to form their own prides. By 2018, there were a hundred lions living in Selinda.

The Jouberts made a film called *Birth of a Pride* to show what can happen when lions have a safe place to live, grow, and raise their cubs.

Lion Guardians

Keeping lions safe from hunters isn't the only way to protect them. We also need to pay attention to the problems that can arise when people and lions live too close to each other. Dr. Leela Hazzah and Dr. Stephanie Dolrenry have been working to solve some of those problems. They have help from the Lion Guardians.

When she was a girl, Leela Hazzah spent summer nights on the flat roof of her family's home in Egypt. She listened to her father and uncles tell stories of lions roaring in the night.

But she herself never heard a single lion. At last, her father told her that lions had gone extinct in Egypt. Leela decided that someday she would hear lions herself.

In 2007, Hazzah and Dolrenry, both biologists, founded the Lion Guardians. This organization is based in Kenya and works with Maasai communities to lower the number of lions killed in revenge for preying on their cows, goats, and sheep.

Maasai ranchers rely on the animals they own—their livestock—to provide meat and milk for their families. And if a family needs something (to pay for a doctor, say) they will often sell one of their animals. The livestock are like money in a bank, there to help in an emergency. Because livestock are so valuable,

*Many Maasai families depend on their livestock,
like this cow and calf, for survival.*

having a big herd makes a rancher respected and important.

When lions attack a rancher's animals, their family loses a source of food, wealth, and respect. It's traditional for warriors to track down and kill a lion who takes one of their animals. Maasai warriors with the courage and skill to hunt lions are admired.

Keeping all of this in mind, Hazzah and Dolrenry began the first Lion Guardian program in Kenya. They hired respected Maasai warriors, paying them a hundred dollars a month to become Guardians.

One of a Guardian's jobs is to talk to others in the community, convincing them not to hunt lions even if the lions attack their livestock. The Guardians explain that lions are actually good for a community, bringing in visitors who spend money and create jobs. If lions are killed, those jobs disappear.

Guardians also explain that they can protect livestock without hunting lions. They help to build strong corrals to keep lions away. If a cow or a sheep or a goat gets lost, Guardians do their best to find it before it becomes food for a lion. And Guardians keep track of lions, warning ranchers to stay away from areas where a pride is hunting.

The story of a lion named Nempusel shows how effective Lion Guardians can be.

Nempusel, a young lioness looking for a place to give birth to her cubs, crossed the boundaries of Amboseli National Park in Kenya and found a spot that happened to be near several Maasai homes. A boy who was watching over his grazing animals came too close to the cubs, and Nempusel attacked him. The boy survived, but he had to go to a hospital for care.

Nempusel hadn't just put a community's animals in danger. She'd actually injured a child. She was just the kind of lion that would normally have been hunted down and killed.

Instead, Lion Guardians decided to remove Nempusel and her cubs from the area. Both the mother and cubs were put to sleep with tranquilizer darts and moved inside Amboseli Park. But a few days later, Nempusel reappeared. She'd carried her young cubs over twelve miles, back to the place where she'd given birth to them.

Instead of trying to move the lions again, the Lion Guardians watched them day and night, making sure everyone knew to stay away from the places Nempusel was hunting. Nempusel did manage to slip away and kill one cow, but she did no other damage. And after a while, she took her cubs back inside Amboseli Park. The hard work of the Lion Guardians had kept livestock, lions, and humans safe.

Living Walls

There's another way to make sure that livestock and lions stay apart—a fence. A really good fence.

Dr. Laly Lichtenfeld is the co-founder and CEO of African People & Wildlife. Just as Dr. Hazzah and Dr. Dolrenry did, she set out to reduce the threat to lions that comes from revenge killings.

In traditional Maasai homes, livestock are kept in corrals made by cutting and piling up dried acacia bushes. These thorny walls are strong enough to keep animals in—but not strong enough to keep a hungry lion out.

Lichtenfeld and her team, including many members of the Maasai community, found that they could use African myrrh trees as posts and connect them with chain-link fencing to create a barrier that lions and other predators could not climb or break through. They call their fencing "Living Walls."

Why not just use chain-link fencing by itself? Because it doesn't do as good a job. A small lion or leopard can climb a chain-link fence. Hyenas can dig underneath. But as the African myrrh trees grow, their branches create a barrier above the top of the metal fence, blocking predators from climbing or jumping over it. And the chain-link fence goes deep into the ground, keeping hyenas at bay.

Lichtenfeld and her team work with the communities across northern Tanzania to protect livestock and conserve wildlife with Living Walls. Since their work started, no lions have been killed in homes with Living Walls.

FUN FACTS ABOUT LIONS

1. A lion's roar can be as loud as a crack of thunder.

2. The male lions who live in Tsavo, Kenya, do not have any manes. Scientists are not sure why. Maybe it's a way for the lions to keep cooler.

3. Lions are very similar to tigers except for the color of their fur. If you shaved a lion and a tiger, it would take an expert to tell them apart. (It's true that tigers tend to be bigger than lions—but not *much*

bigger. A large lion might outweigh a small tiger.)

4. A male lion can eat a quarter of his own body weight in one meal.

5. Are you a fan of *The Lion King*? Simba, the name of the main character, means "lion" in Swahili, a language spoken in many African countries.

6. Lions who live in the Kalahari Desert in southern Africa have been known to eat melons. The juice inside the fruit is a valuable liquid in such a dry place.

7. The longest teeth in a lion's mouth are between three and four inches—about half the length of an unsharpened pencil.

8. Sometimes researchers who study lions in the wild carry umbrellas. Lions can be

scared off by an umbrella that opens up suddenly, especially if it's painted with a pair of big, staring eyes.

9. Lions, like other cats, have claws that can be drawn back inside their paws. This means that the claws don't get dull from rubbing on hard ground or rough rock. (The only cat whose claws don't do this is the cheetah. Cheetahs have claws like a dog's that stay out all the time.)

10. If you have a pet cat, you've probably noticed that it spends a lot of time sleeping. Lions are the same. They can spend twenty out of twenty-four hours snoozing.

11. Lions are the only cats alive today that spend their lives in prides. But some scientists think that saber-toothed cats,

who lived in North and South America until they went extinct around ten thousand years ago, may also have lived in groups.

12. Some male lions have blond manes, some have brown ones, and some manes are almost black. One study showed that female lions seem to prefer males with darker manes.

13. If you look into the eyes of a house cat, you'll see that its pupils close into vertical slits. Lions, on the other hand, have round pupils a lot like a human being's.

14. In the wild, female lions may survive until seventeen or eighteen years old, but it's rare for a male to live past twelve. Lions in zoos may live to be a few years older.

15. Young male lions start growing their manes when they are about one year old.

16. Cave lions didn't have manes as big as the lions of today, but males might have had small ruffs of fur around the neck. How do we know what they looked like when they've been extinct for thousands of years? Prehistoric humans made paintings of them that can still be seen on cave walls today.

HOW YOU CAN HELP SAVE THE LIONS

There are a lot of things you can do to help save lions. Here are a few of them.

1. Find out more about lions and big cats in general. The more you learn, the more you'll be excited to make a safe world for these amazing animals. Here are a few books and a film to get you started:

Big Cats
by Seymour Simon

Face to Face with Lions
by Beverly and Dereck Joubert

Lions
by Valerie Bodden

Birth of a Pride
by Beverly and Dereck Joubert

2. Tell people what you know about lions. Do a report for school, or let your family and friends know how fascinating lions are. The more people know about these big cats, the more they'll want to save them, too.

3. Donate some money to organizations that are working to create a safe world for lions. National Geographic Society's Big Cat Conservation project supports many scientists and activists who are doing good work for lions and other big cats. You can find out more about them at NationalGeographic.org/BigCats.

4. Get together with some friends, your class at school, or a group like a Girl Scout or BSA troop, and make even more money to help lions. You could raise funds by holding a bake sale, mowing lawns, shoveling driveways, or creating a coupon that you can sell, offering to do chores around the house. Or you could make some lion art and sell it to family and friends.

5. Learn more about lions by visiting a zoo or wildlife park. While you're there, take a good look at the place (the habitat) where the lions are living. Is it large enough? Big cats need a lot of space. Do the lions have interesting things to do, maybe balls to chase or trees to climb? One zoo sprayed dried leaves with a pumpkin-spice scent and found that their lions enjoyed rolling around in the pile. Dung from prey animals like a zebra can fascinate lions. Don't worry if the lions in the zoo seem pretty sleepy. But look and see if they have things to do when they do wake up. If you think the lions need a better habitat, you can write to the people at the zoo and ask them to make changes.

6. For your next birthday, ask for a lion! (Not a real one.) The World Wildlife Fund will let you or someone in your family "adopt" a lion by making a donation. The donation even comes with an adoption certificate and a cuddly stuffed lion. Tell your family that protecting endangered

animals like lions would be the best gift you can imagine.

7. Explain to people that you know that they should never buy anything made from lion skin or fur, or jewelry that uses lion teeth or claws. Selling lion teeth, claws, and skin is a major reason that people poach lions. If nobody anywhere buys things like this, no one will kill lions to make money.

REFERENCES

"Asiatic Lion Facts." The Zoological Society of London. Accessed April 14, 2022. zsl.org/asiatic-lion-facts.

Dell'Amore, Christine. "'Living Walls' Stop Lions from Attacking Livestock in Tanzania." Animals. National Geographic Society, December 2, 2014. nationalgeographic.com/animals/article /141202-bomas-lions-africa-animals -science-living-walls.

Denis-Huot, Christine, and Michel Denis-Huot.

The Art of Being a Lion. New York: Friedman/Fairfax, 2002.

Divyabhanusinh. "Junagadh State and Its Lions: Conservation in Princely India, 1879–1947." *Conservation & Society* 4, no. 4 (December 2006): 522-540. jstor.org /stable/26392860.

Dunn, Meghan. "Transforming Lion Killers into 'Lion Guardians.'" *CNN*, December 5, 2015. cnn.com/2014/07/24/world /cnnheroes-hazzah/index.html.

"India's Wandering Lions: Asiatic Lion Fact Sheet." *Nature*. PBS, April 14, 2016. pbs.org/wnet/nature/indias-wandering -lions-asiatic-lion-fact-sheet/14129.

Ingraham, Christopher. "Rich American Tourists Kill Hundreds of Lions Each

Year, and It's All Legal." *Washington Post*,
July 29, 2015. washingtonpost.com/news
/wonk/wp/2015/07/29/rich-american
-tourists-kill-hundreds-of-lions-each-year
-and-its-all-legal.

The IUCN Red List of Threatened Species™.
"Lion." Accessed January 5, 2022.
iucnredlist.org/species/15951/115130419.

Joubert, Beverly, and Dereck Joubert. *Birth of
a Pride*. Wildlife Films, 2018. wildlifefilms
.co/birth-of-a-pride.

Lichtenfeld, Laly. "Finding the Balance for
People and Nature." TEDx Talks. You-
Tube. November 11, 2016. youtube.com
/watch?v=fNTgFUu_gic.

Lion Guardians (website). Accessed January
12, 2022. lionguardians.org.

National Geographic Society. "Animals: Photo
Ark: African Lion." Accessed January 6,
2022. nationalgeographic.com/animals
/mammals/facts/african-lion.

National Geographic Society. "Animals: Photo
Ark: Asiatic Lion." Accessed February 2,
2022. nationalgeographic.com/animals
/mammals/facts/asiatic-lion?loggedin
=true.

"Roaring Success: Population of Asiatic
Lions in India Up 29% in 5 Years." *Times
of India*. June 11, 2020. timesofindia
.indiatimes.com/india/roaring-success
-population-of-asiatic-lions-in-india-up-29
-in-5-years/articleshow/76311768.cms.

San Diego Zoo Wildlife Alliance. "Animals:
Lion." San Diego Zoo Wildlife Alliance

Animals & Plants. Accessed November 10,
2021. animals.sandiegozoo.org/animals
/lion.

Schiffman, Richard. "Lion Killing in Tanzania Reduced by Installation of 'Living
Wall' Fences." *Guardian*, April 7, 2014.
theguardian.com/environment/2014
/apr/07/lion-killing-tanzania-reduced
-installation-living-wall-fences-masai.

Smithsonian's National Zoo & Conservation
Biology Institute. "Animals A–Z: Lion."
Acessed November 10, 2021. nationalzoo
.si.edu/animals/lion.

Tucker, Abigail. "The Truth about Lions."
Smithsonian Magazine, January 2010.
smithsonianmag.com/science-nature
/the-truth-about-lions-11558237.

Wildlife Conservation Society. "Wildlife: Lions." Accessed November 19, 2021. wcs.org/our-work/species/lions.

Wildlife Films (website). Accessed February 2, 2022. wildlifefilms.co.

World Wildlife Fund for Nature-India. "Our Work: Priority Species: Threatened Species: Asiatic Lion." World Wildlife Fund. Accessed April 14, 2022. wwfindia.org /about_wwf/priority_species/threatened _species/asiatic_lion.

SARAH L. THOMSON has published more than thirty books, including prose and poetry, fiction and nonfiction, picture books, and novels. Her work includes two adventures featuring a teenage-girl ninja, a riveting survival story about wildfires and wombats, and nonfiction about elephants, sharks, tigers, plesiosaurs, saber-toothed cats, and other fascinating creatures. *School Library Journal* called Sarah's picture book *Cub's Big World* "a big must-have." *The Bulletin of the Center for Children's Books* described her novel *Deadly Flowers* as "clever, dangerous, vivacious," and *Booklist* said this fantasy set in feudal Japan is "genuinely thrilling, with surprises at every turn and a solid emotional core." *Deadly Flowers* also received Wisconsin's Elizabeth Burr/Worzalla award. Sarah worked as an editor at HarperCollins and Simon & Schuster before becoming a full-time writer. She lives in Portland, Maine.

Learn more about her work at
SarahLThomson.com

CHELSEA CLINTON is the author of the #1 *New York Times* bestseller *She Persisted: 13 American Women Who Changed the World*; *She Persisted Around the World: 13 Women Who Changed History*; *She Persisted in Sports: American Olympians Who Changed the Game*; *Don't Let Them Disappear: 12 Endangered Species Across the Globe*; *It's Your World: Get Informed, Get Inspired & Get Going!*; *Start Now!: You Can Make a Difference*; with Hillary Clinton, *Grandma's Gardens* and *The Book of Gutsy Women: Favorite Stories of Courage and Resilience*; and, with Devi Sridhar, *Governing Global Health: Who Runs the World and Why?* She is also the Vice Chair of the Clinton Foundation, where she works on many initiatives, including those that help empower the next generation of leaders. She lives in New York City with her husband, Marc, their children and their dog, Soren.

Photo courtesy of the author

You can follow Chelsea Clinton on Twitter
@ChelseaClinton
or on Facebook at
Facebook.com/ChelseaClinton

DON'T MISS MORE BOOKS IN THE

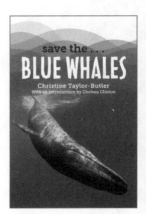

save the . . .
BLUE WHALES
Christine Taylor-Butler
With an introduction by Chelsea Clinton

save the . . .
ELEPHANTS
Sarah L. Thomson
With an introduction by Chelsea Clinton

save the . . .
FROGS
Sarah L. Thomson
With an introduction by Chelsea Clinton

save the . . .
LIONS
Sarah L. Thomson
With an introduction by Chelsea Clinton

save the . . .
POLAR BEARS
Christine Taylor-Butler
With an introduction by Chelsea Clinton

save the . . . SERIES!

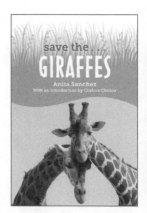

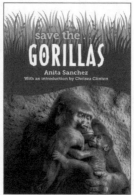

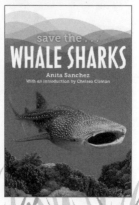